Phases of Lily

Also by Amna Dhanani

My Existence Craves Yours

You were the Soul to my Existence

Phases of Lily

Amna Dhanani

www.amnadhanani.com
Instagram: **amnadhanani_**
Facebook page: **amnadhanani/**
Twitter: **AmnaDhanani_**

Copyright © 2020

By Amna Dhanani
All Rights Reserved.
No part of this book may be reproduced or used in any manner without the express written permission of the publisher except the use of brief quotations in a book review.

ISBN 978-1-949773-04-0
Ebook ISBN 978-1-949773-06-4

Cover vision by **Amna Dhanani**
Brought to life by **Sabinaka**
Editing by **S. H. Kazmi**

About the Book

Phases of Lily is a poetry collection filled with emotions of loss, longing, life and lessons in this particular order. Journey of a lifetime within a few words.

Sometimes the pain has to come out the way it is and be shared as it is for it to be lessened.

May this book be able to acknowledge your anger, sorrow, confusion, helplessness and anguish.

Contents

Loss 1
Longing 29
Life 57
Lessons 85

Acknowledgments

Dear Reader,
If you feel more than others,
Know that it's completely okay.

If you're going through pain,
Know that I've been through it too.

If what you're facing seems to have no end,
Know that I got through it, so can you.

There's something you might not be aware of,
Without you knowing, you have been
The reason of my sanity and survival.

I am who I am
Because you listened to what I had to say.

As a token of appreciation,
I dedicate this book to you.

Loss

Amna Dhanani

Perfect Dream

Hold me for tonight and don't let go.
If you must leave, then leave when I'm asleep
Because when I wake up,
I will remember you just as a dream.

– What a perfect dream

Phases of Lily

<u>Gone</u>

You crushed my dreams
But that wasn't enough
So you even took the pieces with you.

Amna Dhanani

Tragedy

They say, to fix a relationship,
There has to be love between a couple
But I loved you and you loved me
And still, it didn't work out.

Heartbreak

We all forget what love looks like
When heartbreak nests a home in our chests.

Naivety

I always knew better than to be with you
But my heart didn't.

Phases of Lily

Irony

Closure is supposed to set you free
But for closure,
I hung in there instead of trying to let go.

Why does irony have to be the one
To teach me lessons, isn't pain enough?

Amna Dhanani

Invisible

Pain can easily hide in plain sight
Because no one wants to see it.

Bittersweet

The moment I feel like
I can't live without a certain person,
My life teaches me
How to live without them.

Amna Dhanani

Bff

Yes, I'm upset.
I'm upset because you don't call anymore.

I'm upset because
We were supposed to be friends forever.

I'm upset because
You're okay with us not being okay.

I'm upset because
Your child will never learn my name.

I'm upset because
I had to delete all the pictures.

I'm upset because
I never get to see your face now.

I'm upset because
Our memories still make me cry.

I'm upset because
You're no longer my best friend.

– 5 years and counting.

Hurt

You were the only one
Who wasn't supposed to hurt me, you know?

Destruction

You came into my life as hope but now,
All I see is ruins of my soul.

– Friends can cost you a lot too

Grief

The grief of a dying friendship is unlike any I've ever known.

Amna Dhanani

<u>Lost Beauty</u>

Sunsets don't look as beautiful without you.

Crumbled

They say, don't let anyone break you but the only ones that have the power to are those who you love. You can choose to leave behind those who don't love you back but what about those who did or still do love you and now chose to break you? How will you not be broken then? And even if you could stop loving although one cannot stop, why would you punish yourself that way?

Anger

I get angry because I care.
The day I become cold,
Your heart will get anxious.

Trust

My life keeps teaching me to not trust people
But I never learn.

Amna Dhanani

Sadness

I grew up with sadness,
Why do they expect happiness in my words?

Phases of Lily

<u>Wish</u>

She's not just a child,
She's a person like you.
She can feel and observe too.

I wish someone had said that
Whenever I was dismissed by those around me.

Amna Dhanani

Wishful Thinking

When I was a child I used to think,
I will get to live once this suffering is over.
I used to think nothing bad would happen to me
Since I haven't even started to live yet.
I didn't realize that was my life then
But now I know, this is how my life is.

– A suffering

Depression

Depression is something that makes you want to work for yourself at the same time when you're working against yourself. Sounds crazy, right? But if you really think about it, it actually motivates you to change what is giving you depression in the first place whether you seek a temporary escape or work towards a solution.

Then slowly, there comes a time when things start happening, your efforts actually start to pay off and that scares you, you start self-sabotaging because you realize the change is real.

You like it but you're afraid of losing it, it feels like finding another great love after losing a great love.
You don't think it would be possible but then it happens and you wonder if this disappears too, what am I going to do? So you reject it before it rejects you. Self-love is like that as well.

Depression wants to turn it into self-loathing for everything that is not your fault but comes from you. Self-love is something you need to keep building yourself until you start growing into it and it starts growing inside of you.

It's so much and nothing at all at the same time because it doesn't have a face to it, that's the time when you realize that you have to put what you see in the mirror on that face

But all you're able to see is the you that depression has made dull and weak. The dark circles and wrinkles get too real. You wonder, is it worth it to try and fix this outer version of yourself? And if you are not able to, would you be able to accept it?

Accepting seems like the biggest battle because what you've seen in the movies and books is that once you accept something for what it is, it's all sunshine and rainbows, things start to work out themselves.

In real life, it doesn't work that way because it's not just about your wrinkles, you have to live with your whole body.

After accepting, you have to keep finding ways to live with it, to cope with it.
While your coping mechanisms have been so toxic that you don't know how to deal with reality anymore, much less knowing a healthy way to.

Your immune system gets weakened and everything inside your body changes.
Depression is not just a mental illness, it has many physical symptoms and even if it didn't, your mind keeping your body on bed for too long will cause many problems.

Phases of Lily

These are facts, there's no silver lining I've been able to find yet other than the fact that hope lives with the pain and we need to keep our eyes on hope while we deal with pain. Life has so much to offer to give up for anything.

Unjust World

We live in a world where we are blamed
For feeling and then,
For expressing how we feel.

Darkness

The quiet nights scare me
Instead of offering peace.

Nightmares

They ask me what do I dream of?
I dream about me, being far away across the ocean, contemplating a bigger escape from my life than the one I'm already at.
And realizing that I drag the things with me I desire to escape from. The consequences of my decisions and the responsibilities I have, I've carried them here with me.

– I dream nightmares

Longing

Amna Dhanani

Yearn

When I spoke to him,
He chose to look at my lips and not my eyes.

Honesty

I've tasted many lies
Before I got to taste your lips.

Almost

You're more than a distant memory,
You're something that almost never happened
But that almost is the reason I still suffer.

Agony

Your absence makes my soul ache,
I refuse to believe that
You had only touched my heart with your love.

Desire

I crave your existence to the point
My own existence crumbles into dust,
Ready to be blown away
By a soft whisper of the wind.
And I desperately wish
If my end has to come
That whisper becomes you.

Album

You're nothing but an album of memories
Sometimes I can't find
And other times I don't want to see.

Amna Dhanani

<u>Memories</u>

The shadow of your memories
Follows me everywhere.

Time

It will take me a while to not want you at all.

Amna Dhanani

Motherhood

In me, aches the heart of a mother,
A mother, who doesn't have a child yet.

Heartache

Whenever I hear someone's child crying,
It tears my heart apart.
I wonder what it does to their own mother.

Amna Dhanani

Contentment

His tiny heart against my heart,
He fell asleep in my arms.
What a little miracle he is, I thought
And wished one for myself
As I handed him back to his mother.

Broken Heart

He wasn't mine to keep
But my heart broke as his little fingers
Were forced to let go of my index finger.

Baby

I'm ready to give my world to someone
Who isn't even in the world yet.

Phases of Lily

Rebirth

I'll be born as a mother
When you're born from me
But the love I have for you
Cannot be contained already
And you're not even in my womb yet.

Amna Dhanani

Prisoner

At times, my body becomes a cage for my soul.
I can't be as liberated as my soul desires to be.

Dependent

Let's think about the grass for one minute,
It only feels liberated
When the wind is kind enough.

Amna Dhanani

Unrecognized

You're an apostrophe,
Necessary and admired.
I'm a comma,
They need me to pause
Yet no one pauses enough
To realize its worth.

Phases of Lily

Pictures

I want to write about why I don't take pictures anymore but I know it won't stop there.
The thought that this moment won't last haunts me.

The picture becomes a prized possession that I never look at in fear that it will remind me of what I had, yet it won't retrieve what I felt back then, if I felt anything at all, because at that time, when I'm trying to capture the moment in my mind, my heart and in a camera, I'm trying to feel what I should be feeling which is already escaping me.

I have no words to explain that every circle of life no matter how big or small has become vicious.

Special moments don't feel special.
Anything that has been written on them what should be felt at that time gives no feeling to me, not even slightly.
For example, excitement. It's like I'm numb.
Happiness means that I acknowledge something good is happening, happiness is not a feeling for me anymore, it's an acknowledgement.

Big things pass me by, I feel empty.
Small things and details that I used to live for pass me by, and I feel nothing.

Is this a coma that you cannot wake up from?

Amna Dhanani

It's like the part of you that feels is paralyzed.
I don't think my heart is numb but paralyzed.
It senses but it doesn't feel and God forbid, if it
ever comes close to feeling, I feel the fear of not
feeling first and there, in a millisecond, it's gone,
the feeling and the fear both.

I can't even feel pain the way it should be felt, I
acknowledge it as something that happens every
day and is a routine that I can't escape from and
have stopped trying to, to be honest. Even the
freaking pain doesn't shock me in any way,
whether it's new and unexpected or old and
deepened.

So why should I take pictures?
Trying for a perfect click?
Waste seconds for something I am too exhausted
to do, something that doesn't benefit me,
something instead of cherishing,
I just lock away in phone storage and later on
somewhere in a drive on the laptop so that my
phone has space for more pictures.
I'd rather try to feel and later on forget than try
to capture what was never meant to be captured,
a moment that needs to be felt.

Phases of Lily

Traumatic Childhood

They said I was allowed to make friends
But I had to be home-schooled.

They said I was allowed to make friends
But not allowed to go to their place.

They said I was allowed to make friends
But not allowed to keep in touch via phone.

They said I was allowed to make friends
But not allowed to have them over.

If somehow,
I had gotten someone to play with me,
They'd say I was allowed to play with them
As long as I stayed within their sight,
Just a few steps away from the house
With an invisible leash
But hey, I was allowed to make friends, right?

– Overprotectiveness keeps you safe and kills you at the same time

Amna Dhanani

<u>Twisted</u>

I'm a girl who desperately wants to be loved
In a home that loves her too much.

Lost

A house empty of love
Is a garden where thorns bloom.
Every mouth is like a pair of scissors
Waiting to cut open your wounds.
When we are hurt, we all crawl back
To a place called home
But when it's your home you run away from,
Where do the wandering souls go?

Amna

My name means peace
But I don't belong with it.

Loneliness

The moon taunts me through the clouds,
As if she's saying,
I have clouds tonight,
Who do you have?

Amna Dhanani

<u>Void</u>

Sometimes I revisit our past,
Not because I miss you or I'm not over you
But because I'm lonely.
It was easier to get through day by day,
Night by night, with your pain in my heart.
I was used to the company
But now that my heart is empty,
Sometimes the void gets too much to bear.

Life

Amna Dhanani

<u>Alive</u>

The sun had to kiss my eyelids
To make me realize, I'm still alive.

Phases of Lily

Fleeting Happiness

I think this notion has been stuck in my mind
ever since I watched this black and white
Indian movie.
How old was I? Eight? Seven?
I honestly cannot remember.

All I can remember now is that there was a
beggar who never had a good or a proper meal
in his life. He met a very kind and generous
man, who handed him a thousand rupees.
The beggar went to a restaurant after dressing up
and ordered everything on the menu. When all
the food arrived, he just stared at the dishes in
awe and just froze.
The waiter came out and then I realized that the
poor man had passed away because he could not
handle so much happiness.
So after watching this, my mind of a child knew
why me and my family didn't get all the
happiness we deserved all at once, because we
would not be able to handle it.

As I grew up, many things got added into this
belief because of my experiences
Because of how I felt even with one big news in
my hands at a time, it was so hard to control my
happiness. I'd end up in tears every time even
with little joys. I started to suppress happiness
with so many reasons that I find to be invalid
now despite some of them being true.

Amna Dhanani

I didn't want to feel it all because then,
It would be finished.

I didn't want to feel it all because then
something terrible would happen.

I didn't want to feel it all because
I was craving for more good things to happen
while I hadn't even digested this one and didn't
want to either.

I didn't want my tank to be full for the next one.

And a few other reasons that I cannot think of
right now.

Slowly, happiness started to feel less and less.
Sometimes because of the shock and
suddenness,

Sometimes because I was numb,

Sometimes because the sorrow had engulfed me
before happiness could.

Sometimes because happiness didn't look like
what I thought it would look like

And sometimes it just didn't feel like what I had
hoped and prayed for.

Now I can't remember what it felt like,
the true happiness, the big one, the huge one.

Phases of Lily

I remember its face being there somewhere in
the recent past but I don't remember the feel of
it. And I'm craving, I'm craving it so much and it
feels like I'm dying without it and yet,
I continue to breathe.

Amna Dhanani

Hopeful

I'm the only one who knows
Every dark pit inside of me and yet, I'm hopeful.

Straightforward

I'm a bad person
Because I see the truth as it is
And deliver it as it is.

Impression

Success does not impress me, personality does.

Phases of Lily

?

Sometimes when we keep looking for answers,
Our life becomes a big question mark.

Normalcy

There's no normalcy but different perceptions
Of what it's supposed to be.

Phases of Lily

Beauty

Sometimes we just see what we want to see.
For example when the sun sets,
Some people think of it as sadness, an ending.
And some people think of it as hope,
As a promise of a better tomorrow
When it rises again.
Then there's people like me,
What I see is another face of beauty.

Amna Dhanani

Secret

There's a secret relationship between the sun
And the water which no one talks about.

Transparency

Talk to me like the sky talks to the water openly
And the water reflects back
Every word in the form of beauty.

– Honesty is beauty for me

Amna Dhanani

Disappointment

The temporary escapes in life
Have become so easy and unsatisfying.

Pride

I wonder where does pride come from
When nothing is actually ours,
We own nothing, not even ourselves.
Our bodies belong to Earth
And our souls belong to God.

Amna Dhanani

<u>Fire</u>

Don't ignite a fire in me
If you can't bear the heat.

Basic Right

I offer sincerity, respect and honesty,
These are the base of my existence.
I will give them to you
Whether we have a future together or not.
This is who I am,
I don't give because I want to take
But I don't get involved
With anything less than what I have to offer.
I'm not ashamed of wanting
The most basic things,
I have the right to as a human being.

Amna Dhanani

Closure

Don't become one of those questions
I've learned to live with.
I've had to move on without closure before
And you won't be able to stop me
From doing so again.

Struggle

Even something as fragile as a flower
Needs sunlight to grow.
Just like that,
Every hardship that we face
Is only there to make us stronger.

Amna Dhanani

Storm

If it's true that life prepares you
For what it is to come,
It has to be one hell of a storm.

Silence

I like to stay quiet
Because the world is loud enough.

Amna Dhanani

Anxiety

Crowds make me anxious
But what's worse is a crowded mind.

Relief

I've seen so many people just up and leave
From my life that now if someone does that,
I'm actually relieved that
It was sooner than later, instead of being sad.

Amna Dhanani

Uncertainty

I don't know
When to accept what I'm given as blessings
Because they can be taken away
If not appreciated.

And

I don't know when to keep fighting for more
Because I shouldn't be settling
For less than what I deserve.

– What my mother taught me vs what life did

Untamed Beast

She's an untamed beast,
You shouldn't expect flowers in her hair
Just because she's a her.

Meaningless

My heart has been to many places
But it has never been
In unnecessary conversations.

Lessons

Quarantine

Life stays still, time flies.

<u>War</u>

Wars change us all, whether it's a world war
Or the war of the world within.

The Becoming

This part in my life isn't called suffering,
It's called shaping.
My life is turning me into the person
I deserve to be.

Respect

Manners apply to elders as well.

Family

Those who hurt you on purpose, aren't family.

Lesson

Never take me for granted,
I've learned it the hard way
But I've learned to leave.

Amna Dhanani

Sensitive

When I point out how wrong are the ways
In which, they speak to me,
I get told that I'm too sensitive.
Before it used to make me angry
But now I smile and say
"Yes, I'm glad that I am sensitive,
Otherwise I wouldn't be able to understand
How wrong it is to talk this way."

Shine

Some are afraid of spiders
And some keep them as pets.
Don't let anyone bully you for having fears
Or for standing out in a crowd.
You are unique and beautiful,
And you deserve to shine as who you are.

Amna Dhanani

Reminder

To fight any calamity,
You need to make the right decisions.

To make the right decisions,
You need to stay calm.

To stay calm,
You need to reassure yourself with positivity.

Make a positive loop in your head
Instead of a negative one

As a human mind
Goes from emotion to action,
Then from action to emotion,
Which becomes a loop.

Keeping a positive mindset
Is very important for anything and everything.

Positive Message

The sun doesn't stay gone forever.
The stars never stop shining.
The moon is always full.
It's all about the timing.

Amna Dhanani

Priceless

Living has a cost
Which cannot be paid with money.

The Truth

You left my side to strengthen your own.
I wish I could blame you
But I know that in the end,
We always serve ourselves more.

Healing

I've healed from things I never thought
I'd make it out of alive.
For once I can say,
Pain has shaped me
Instead of only leaving scars behind.

Seeking Solace

When a mother punishes her child,
He still runs to her for comfort.
Just like that, when someone breaks our heart,
We automatically run
To the same person to mend it,
That's a mistake one should never make.

Amna Dhanani

Privacy

You don't have to
Show your happiness for it to be true.

– Peace before pictures

Bound

You're never free,
Everything you do has a ripple effect.

Rock Bottom

Never say you've hit rock bottom
Because life takes it as a challenge
And throws you down deeper.

Misunderstood

I believe silence is the most misunderstood,
Not words.

Amna Dhanani

Still

Not going anywhere takes you places too.

Trauma

While I was trained for not letting anyone down,
The only person I ever let down was myself.

Awareness

Everything is calm when I'm aware
Of the chaos within.
The real chaos starts when I'm not self-aware.

Fact

Validation has become an addiction.

I touch your soul with my words
And that for me, is love.

Thank you for allowing me to feel it

About the Author

Amna Dhanani, now an author whose poetry is read around the world, hails from a small town in Sindh, Pakistan. Her journey started when she was 11 with an article she wrote inspired by her mother. The praise she received for this article gave birth to a writer in her with the sole purpose of touching souls.

Amna has only attended school till 8th grade; however, her passion to learn and pursue the creative journey has paved the way for her. She is self-taught, passionate and a diligent writer who has specialized the art of speaking volumes in a few words.

Her keen observation of the world is the reason she has been able to stand against the unjust norms in the society. She is now breaking stereotypes and speaking about topics that are left undiscussed. In her two previous poetry books, My Existence Craves Yours and You were the Soul to My Existence, she talks about her perception of various shades of this world including love, pain, mental health and heartbreaks of many kinds.

Amna has become a voice for those who struggle and teaches the wisdom required for survival.

www.ingramcontent.com/pod-product-compliance
Lightning Source LLC
Chambersburg PA
CBHW051346040426
42453CB00007B/433